# UNSTUCK AND UNSTOPPABLE

*The One Image Method to Break Free from Overwhelm and Achieve Your Dreams*

BY

## ERIC HAWKINS

# TABLE OF CONTENTS

# INTRODUCTION
# Scrolling Through Someone Else's Life

You're sitting there, phone in hand, with no real intention beyond passing time. The screen lights up, pulling you in.

First, it's a picture of someone's vacation—an influencer basking in the sun, toes buried in pristine sand, the sand you've only seen in travel brochures. You pause for a moment, mesmerized by the turquoise water behind her.

The algorithm takes over.

Next comes a shot of a sleek, shiny car—precisely the one you saved as wallpaper years ago when dreaming felt like a possibility. You swipe up. Now it's a family photo: coordinated outfits, golden-hour lighting, everyone grinning as if their lives are as perfect as this snapshot suggests.

Swipe. Another friend is on a mountaintop, arms stretched wide, with a caption about finding freedom. Swipe. Someone else just announced their promotion, their achievement shining brightly through your dimly lit screen.

The photos blur together. You don't even realize how much time has passed, the minutes folding into one another like pages of a book you're not sure you want to finish.

For a moment, you're lost—not in the beauty of what you see, but in the quiet sting of what you're *not*.

Your chest tightens. Not because you're jealous—at least that's what you tell yourself—but because every post feels like a reminder of something you once wanted, something you've convinced yourself you can no longer have.

You tell yourself, *Just one more swipe*. And then another.

Before you know it, you're caught in a trance, scrolling through a collage of other people's lives.

# The Ache of Feeling Scattered

But it's not just what you're seeing—it's what it represents.

A life that seems out of reach. Dreams you've shelved for "someday." The nagging feeling that you're falling behind while everyone else seems to be racing ahead.

The notifications blur. The likes, the captions, the comments—they all blend into an endless stream of noise. But beneath it all, there's a voice. A whisper that asks, *Why not me?*

Finally, you snap out of it. You close the app, your thumb lingering over the screen as if it holds all the answers. But as the phone's glow fades, you're left with the same reality as before.

The same pile of laundry.

The identical unopened mail.

The same walls that feel like they've been closing in for years.

And in that moment, a wave of emotion washes over you: frustration, resignation, a quiet, aching sadness.

It's not just the time you've lost to scrolling—it's the feeling of being stuck in a life you didn't choose but don't know how to change.

You tell yourself it's because you're too busy. Too tired. Too late.

But deep down, you know the truth: It's not that you're not trying. It's that your energy is scattered—spread thin across a thousand worries, distractions, and competing goals.

## The Seed of Change

But what if it didn't have to be this way?

What if you could focus all your energy on *one* Vision instead of chasing dozens of scattered goals?

A vision is so clear, so vivid that it pulls you forward— even on the hard days.

What if that Vision wasn't just an idea in your head but something you could see, feel, and carry with you daily?

We are not talking about a traditional vision board cluttered with pictures of every dream you've ever had. We are talking about **the One-Image Method**—a simple yet powerful tool that captures everything you genuinely want in **an Image**.

Here's what makes this different:

Your One Image isn't just a picture on a wall. It's a roadmap, a guide, and a visual anchor that connects your goals, your purpose, and your daily actions into one cohesive, unstoppable force.

It simplifies your decisions, narrows your focus, and gives you the clarity you've been searching for. Because when you know exactly what you're working toward, everything else falls into place.

This book isn't about doing more. It's about doing what *matters*. It's about cutting through the noise, finding your focus, and finally moving forward with purpose and direction.

## You Are Not Alone

If this sounds familiar, let me stop here and tell you something important: **You are not alone.**

Feeling stuck is a universal experience, though few people talk about it. You might think everyone else has it all figured out—that they're happier, more successful, more fulfilled. But the truth is, many people are sitting exactly where you are, silently asking the same questions:

1.   Why does it feel like no matter how hard I try, I'm still in the same place?

2.   What's wrong with me? Why can't I make it work?

3.   Am I the only one who feels this way?

You're not.

Feeling stuck doesn't mean you're failing. It doesn't mean you're broken or incapable. It means you're human. It's a sign that something in your life no longer fits—a signal that you're ready for something *more*.

## The Invitation

This book is your invitation to stop settling for *almost* and start reaching for *unstoppable*.

Through **The One Image Method** and the **PATH Framework**, you'll learn how to clarify your Vision, align your actions, and create a fulfilling and purpose-driven life.

When you turn the final page, you won't just have a dream but a roadmap. And more importantly, you'll have the confidence and tools to bring that Vision to life.

So take a deep breath. Close the apps. Let go of the noise.

It's time to stop scrolling through someone else's life and start building your own.

Let's begin.

# CHAPTER 1:
# Rethinking Hard Work

*"The only place success comes before work is in the dictionary."*
— *Vidal Sassoon*

*"Working hard is noble, but working hard without knowing where you're going is like running a race with no finish line—exhausting and directionless. Define your path, then let your effort have a purpose."*
— *Eric Hawkins*

## What Does Hard Work Really Mean?

Oh, I know hard work. I've known it my whole life.

Growing up on a farm, my days were full of chores that couldn't wait. The chickens had to be fed without fail, and let me tell you, those birds were loud if you were even a minute late. The hogs weren't much better—they needed feeding, too, and cleaning their pens was an entirely different beast of a task. For a while, we had cows, and they added another layer of responsibility.

If you've never carried buckets of water that you had to hand pump, lugged them to the hog pen, and poured the water into the trough only to watch the hogs waste half of it on the ground—you haven't lived the whole farm experience.

And then there were the vegetables. Our fields grew corn, tomatoes, cucumbers, butter beans, collards, and more, depending on the season. Those plants didn't care if it was 100 degrees outside or you were tired from school. They needed watering, weeding, and, eventually, harvesting. If you didn't stay on top of it, weeds would overrun the crops, and all your earlier efforts would go to waste.

The work—or my father—never asked if I was tired, wanted a break or was in the mood to do it. It just had to get done.

## The Purpose and Direction of Farm Work

But here's the thing about being raised on a farm: **no work was without purpose and direction.** Every task had a clear reason behind it, which kept me going, even when the work felt endless.

When you fed the chickens, you knew it was so they would lay eggs that we could eat or sell. Tending to the hog pens wasn't glamorous, but it kept the animals healthy, which meant they'd grow strong enough to take to market. Harvesting vegetables wasn't just about pulling food from the ground—it was about providing for our family and earning a living. Every chore was connected to a larger goal, whether small or dirty.

That's the difference. Farm work wasn't just busy work. It wasn't about going through the motions to stay occupied. **It was about contributing to something bigger.** You could look out over the rows of corn or watch the hogs grow and know that your effort was building something real, something meaningful.

## A Lesson in Purpose

One summer afternoon, I was drenched in sweat, standing in a field, pulling weeds from between rows of butter beans. I had just finished my work and started walking back toward the house. My head was down, lost in thought.

My father's voice rang out from across the field: *"Hey, boy, come here!"*

I could tell he wasn't in the best mood as I approached. My heart sank—I wasn't sure what I had done wrong. And for those who grew up in the '70s and '80s like I did, you know there's no "safe distance" from your parents. Another state, maybe, but even that was questionable.

When I got close enough, he looked me square in the eye and said, "Boy, don't you ever let me see you walk with your head down again. Ain't nothing down there but the ground. Keep your head up so you can see where you're going. Even if you have nowhere to go, walk like you've got a place to be. Keep your head up—you never know who's watching you."

"Yes, sir... Daddy," I replied.

That moment stuck with me. Daddy wasn't just telling me to lift my head while I walked—he was teaching me to **carry myself with purpose**, even when I wasn't sure of the destination.

## Connecting Hard Work to Vision

Here's the thing: Most of us aren't working with that kind of clarity anymore. Instead of focusing on one clear purpose, we've pulled in a dozen directions, juggling goals, obligations, and distractions.

That's why so many people feel stuck. It's not because they're lazy or incapable—their effort isn't anchored to anything meaningful.

What my father taught me that day wasn't just about walking tall—it was about living tall. He showed me that purpose isn't just about what you're doing; it's about why you're doing it.

Imagine if all your hard work was guided by one clear Vision—your version of success, represented in a powerful image. Every step you take, every decision you make, would be anchored in that one goal.

That's the power of clarity. That's the power of **The One Image Method**.

When your Vision is clear, your hard work becomes meaningful. You're no longer spinning your wheels or wasting energy on things that don't matter—instead, every effort you put in moves you closer to the life you want.

## The Farm vs. the Treadmill

Let's put it another way. Imagine two people working equally hard. One is running on a treadmill, sweat pouring down, legs burning. The other is walking down a dirt road, step by step.

The person on the treadmill is exerting incredible effort, but they're still in the same place at the end of the day. The person walking down the road? They might be moving slower, but they're getting closer to a destination with every step.

Farm work was like walking down that road. Every chore had a direction, a purpose, and a destination. But I've also had moments when my effort felt more like running on a treadmill— exhausting myself without getting anywhere.

And I bet you've had those moments, too.

## Reflection: The Farm's Simple Wisdom

My father used to say, *"The crops don't grow themselves, but they also won't grow if you don't give them space."* This saying reminds me that **hard work must be paired with the right environment, tools, and mindset.**

Here's how this wisdom applies to your everyday life:

1. What is my version of planting the crops?

2.  Are you investing in skills or opportunities that will grow your future? Are you aligning your efforts with your One Image—the Vision representing your deepest goals?

3.  Am I pulling weeds in a field that's going to bear fruit?

4.  Are you spending your time and energy on tasks or relationships that truly matter? Pulling weeds means eliminating distractions and obstacles that prevent you from focusing on what's truly important.

5.  Is the work I'm doing right now contributing to the life I want to build?

6.  Take a close look at your daily routine. Is your hard work building toward a goal, or are you simply staying busy?

7.  Am I creating the right environment for growth?

8.  Like crops, growth needs the right conditions to thrive. Are you surrounding yourself with people, tools, and habits that support your Vision?

9.  Am I giving myself space to rest and reflect?

10. Rest isn't laziness—it's the space where you ensure your hard work is paying off.

## A New Definition of Hard Work

Hard work isn't just about effort. It's about effort with **intention**, knowing where you're going, and why it matters.

When hard work is anchored in purpose and connected to your One Image, it stops feeling like a grind and starts feeling like progress.

This chapter isn't about telling you to work harder. It's about showing you how to work **smarter** with clarity and focus. As you progress, I'll show you how to align every step with the life you truly want to build.

Because the truth is, you don't need more effort. You need more clarity.

Turn the page. Let's take the next step together.

# CHAPTER 2:

# When the Vision Feels Out of Reach

## The Ache of Feeling Stuck

You know what you want—or at least think you do. You've pictured it a thousand times: the life you've worked hard for. You've told yourself, *This is what I want, and I'll do whatever it takes to get there.*

But here you are, and it feels like the dream is still out of reach.

The harder you try, the more it seems to slip away. And the worst part? You can't shake the feeling that maybe—just maybe—you're incapable of achieving it.

It's an exhausting cycle. You work and pour in the energy, yet nothing feels like progress.

If you've ever felt this way, let me say loud and clear: **You are not alone.**

Feeling stuck doesn't mean you're failing. It doesn't mean you're broken or incapable. It means you're human.

## The Invisible Trap of Unfocused Effort

Here's the thing: Most people aren't stuck because they lack effort. They're stuck because their effort is scattered.

Imagine this: You're standing at the center of a field with a watering can. In every direction, there are seeds you've planted—representing your goals, responsibilities, and dreams. You want them all to grow, so you pour a little water here, a little there, running back and forth to cover as much ground as possible.

But no matter how hard you try, none of the seeds seem to sprout.

The water is too spread out, so the seeds aren't getting the consistent care they need to grow.

That's what happens when your energy is divided among too many goals, distractions, and "should-dos." Your effort feels relentless, but without focus, it leads nowhere.

"Too many goals and distractions create confusion."

"Clarity comes from focusing on one powerful image that encapsulates your vision."

## The One Image Solution

Now, imagine a different approach. Instead of running back and forth trying to water every seed, you focus on one—a single, clear image of what matters most.

That's the power of **The One Image Method**.

Creating a vision distilled into a single image is a focal point for your energy and decisions. You're no longer scattering your effort but channeling it toward what truly matters.

## A Story of Evolving Dreams

I remember the day I saw *Cannonball Run*.

The movie opened with a wide-open highway and the mighty roar of an engine that sent chills down my spine. Then came the Image that awed me—a sleek and fierce Lamborghini Countach.

At first glance, it was just a car. But it represented something much bigger: freedom, success, and the ability to create a life on my terms.

As a teenager, I couldn't achieve that dream, but I did what I could—I found a poster of the car and hung it on my wall. It wasn't just decoration. That Image became my guide. It symbolized the kind of life I wanted: a life where I had control over my future and the freedom to enjoy it.

The Vision wasn't just a motivator—it shaped every decision I made. Early on, I understood I had to stay focused to reach that dream.

I learned quickly who I should—and shouldn't—spend time with. I stayed away from distractions like drugs and unhealthy influences that could have pulled me off track.

But it wasn't easy. There were moments when I doubted myself. Times when I felt stuck or tempted to take shortcuts. What kept me going was that Vision above my bed.

Whenever I faced a decision, I asked myself, "*Does this move me closer to the life I want?*" If the answer was no, I walked away.

## The Dream Evolves

By turning 20, I had built a strong foundation for success. I wasn't ready to buy the car yet, but I had achieved something even more significant—I was on the path to a future I had dreamed about for years.

Then, I met Sylvia.

After we married, my dream shifted in a way I hadn't expected. By the age of 21, we had built a 3000-square-foot new home. In the process, I discovered that the dream I had built around the car wasn't the end goal. I realized that I wanted more than material success.

I found something better.

The life Sylvia and I built together became my new dream. It was rich with experiences, purpose, and shared success—things no car could ever give me.

And yet, I could achieve this life because of that original Vision.

## Dreams Evolve Because You Do

Here's what I learned: The Vision you start with isn't always the one you finish with. And that's okay.

Dreams evolve because *you* evolve. What matters is having a clear image to guide you through the moments when you feel stuck or uncertain.

Your dream may not be tied to a car. Perhaps it's about financial peace, travel, or the courage to start fresh.

Whatever it is, find that **One Image** that lights a fire inside you. Let it guide your decisions.

You might not end up exactly where you expected, but you'll create a better life.

Why The One Image Works

**The One Image Method** is so effective in how your brain processes information.

1. Clarity Cuts Through Overwhelm:

2. When goals feel scattered, the brain struggles to prioritize. A single image simplifies focus, making it easier to take action.

3. Your Brain Needs a Target:

4. Neuroscience shows that the brain's Reticular Activating System (RAS) helps filter out distractions and notice what aligns with your goals. When you repeatedly see your One Image, your brain starts recognizing opportunities and connections that move you closer to that Vision.

5. Emotional Anchoring:

6. A clear image creates an emotional connection to your goal. It's not just a list of tasks— it's a visual representation of the life you want, which keeps you motivated even on tough days.

## Making Decisions with Confidence

One of the most potent effects of **The One Image Method** is how it simplifies decision-making.

Think about how much time and energy you spend second-guessing yourself:

1. Should I take this opportunity or wait for something better?

2. Do I focus on this goal or that one?

3. Is this the right time to make a change?

When you have a **One Image**, the answers become more evident.

Every decision can be filtered through a straightforward question:

## Does this move me closer to my Vision?

If the answer is yes, you say yes. If the answer is no, you let it go.

## Your Turn: Creating Your One Image

Let's make this personal.

Close your eyes and imagine the life you want—not just the surface-level goals but the feelings, relationships, and experiences that matter most to you.

Now, ask yourself: What Image captures that life?

It could be a photo of your dream home, a place you've always wanted to visit, or a symbol of success that resonates with you.

Choose one Image that represents your ultimate Vision.

## How to Make It Work

1. **Keep It Simple:** Focus on one Image that encapsulates your main goal.

2. **Place It Everywhere:** Make it your phone background screensaver, or print it out and put it where you'll see it daily.

3. **Use It as Your Filter:** Before making decisions, glance at your Image and ask yourself if your choice aligns with it.

## Hope on the Other Side of Stuck

Feeling stuck is painful, but it's also a signal. It means you're ready for change. And that change begins with clarity.

With **the One-Image Method**, you don't need all the answers immediately. You need direction— a single, powerful vision to guide you.

So, if you're standing in that field, watering every seed and wondering why nothing is growing, stop.

Choose one. Focus your energy. Let the rest fall away.

Because the life you want isn't out of reach; it's waiting for you to stop scattering your effort and start building with intention.

Turn the page. Your transformation starts now.

# CHAPTER 3:
# Focusing on Problems, Not Solutions

*"We cannot solve our problems with the same thinking we used when we created them."*
— *Albert Einstein*

*"Free your mind and your ass will follow."*
— *Funkadelic:*

## Caught in the Loop

Let me ask you something: How much time do you spend thinking about what's wrong in your life?

Think about it.

It could be the frustration of not making enough money, the ache of a stuck relationship, or the regret of missed opportunities. Perhaps it's replaying that one mistake you can't seem to forgive yourself for or the anxiety about an uncertain future.

You wake up in the morning, and before your feet hit the floor, the weight of your problems crashes down on you.

The bills that need to be paid.

The tasks you didn't finish yesterday.

The dream you're chasing that still feels so far away.

The more you dwell on these problems, the heavier they feel.

You tell yourself, *If I can figure this out, everything will get better.* So, you dig in, replaying the same worries over and over in your mind. But instead of finding clarity, you feel even more stuck.

Sound familiar?

I know it does because I've been there.

## The Emotional Trap of Focusing on Problems

Years ago, I lived in this loop. I'd spend hours—days, even—obsessing over everything that wasn't working in my life.

Why wasn't I making more progress?

Why did every decision feel like the wrong one?

Why did it seem like everyone else had it figured out while I was stuck spinning my wheels?

I convinced myself I'd find the answer if I could think, work, or push through. But the more I focused on my problems, the more they consumed me.

I didn't realize then that the more energy you give your problems, the bigger they grow.

## A Story of Overcoming Despair and Finding a Solution

Several years after my wife and I were married, we started a hair salon in Virginia Beach. It was doing well, but my wife had an even bigger dream—a vision that inspired both of us.

She wanted to create a full-scale wellness center where clients could come for hair services, nails, body massages, and fitness. It was ambitious, but we believed in it.

To bring that dream to life, we took out a second mortgage.

The project began with excitement and momentum, but soon, reality hit us like a brick wall. Hidden structural issues and unexpected costs started to pile up, draining our budget faster than we had ever anticipated.

Every new surprise felt like a gut punch. The fitness area, meant to be the centerpiece of the entire facility, became a glaring symbol of our setbacks. We had to cut the equipment budget almost entirely. The most significant part of the salon stood empty—nothing but open space and broken promises.

Customers would ask, *"When are you getting the fitness equipment?"* Every time, I had to force a smile and devise an excuse. Inside, I was panicking.

I lost sleep over it.

People pay good money to visit a wellness center, but how could we meet those expectations with an empty, unfinished space? I would lie awake at night wondering where I would find $50,000 to buy the commercial-grade fitness equipment we needed. We had just $8,000 left for that part of the project, which wouldn't cut it.

I felt stuck—trapped in an endless loop of problems. *This isn't going to work. We're going to fail.* The weight of those thoughts was crushing.

## Shifting to a Solution Mindset

But then something shifted.

One night, I took a deep breath. I told myself I needed to stop obsessing over what was wrong and focus on finding a solution, no matter how impossible it seemed. The moment I made that decision, things started to change.

I sat down with my laptop and started searching.

I knew buying used equipment was an option, but it came with challenges. Used equipment from multiple sources would be mismatched and difficult to maintain. Worse, if I had to settle for home-use models, they wouldn't hold up under daily wear and tear. People wouldn't trust us if the equipment didn't look and feel like it belonged in a high-end wellness center.

But I didn't give up. I kept reminding myself: *There's a solution. I just haven't found it yet.*

I adopted a new approach: "If you can think it, type it." I began searching online not just for used equipment but also for auctions selling fitness equipment.

Eventually, I stumbled across something unexpected— government auction sites. The military was auctioning off commercial-grade fitness equipment from naval ships.

At first, I was skeptical. Would this equipment be in decent shape? Could I even trust the auction process?

I decided to test the waters by bidding on a group of televisions the government was auctioning. The process went smoothly, and I successfully bought the TVs. With that experience under my belt, I felt more confident.

When I found an extensive collection of fitness equipment being auctioned next, I knew this was my moment. I placed my bid and waited.

When I won, I couldn't believe it. For just $5,000—less than what we had left in our budget—I secured everything we needed: commercial-grade treadmills, strength machines, and other equipment that looked like it belonged in any top-tier fitness center.

The relief was overwhelming. All the nights of worry and the endless spiral of doubt had all been worth it. The fitness area was no longer a burden. It became a showpiece. Customers were impressed, business picked up, and my wife's dream was finally coming to life.

# Why Focusing on Problems Keeps You Stuck

If you've been stuck in this cycle, you're not alone. Most of us do it, and there's a reason why:

1. Problems Feel Urgent

2. Problems demand attention. They shout, *Fix me now!* They take over your thoughts and make you feel like you can't move forward until they're resolved.

3. We Mistake Worry for Progress

4. Thinking about your problems is a strange comfort—it feels like you're doing something. But worrying isn't action. It's just spinning your wheels.

5. Fear of the Unknown

6. Shifting your focus to solutions requires change, and change is scary. It forces you to take risks, step into the unknown, and leave the familiar (even if it isn't working).

7. The Weight of Doubt

8. When you focus on your problems for too long, you start to doubt your ability to solve them. You

feel stuck, and that feeling becomes part of your identity.

## The Shift: From Problems to Solutions

Here's the truth: Problems will always exist. Challenges are a part of life. However, how you approach them determines whether you stay stuck or move forward.

When you focus on solutions, everything changes.

The Role of The One-Image Method

This is where **The One Image Method** becomes your most powerful tool.

Your **One Image** acts as a mental pivot point. It redirects your focus from the weight of your problems to the clarity of your dreams.

Instead of worrying about what's wrong, you channel it into what's possible. That's how you break the cycle of self-doubt and start building momentum.

## How to Shift Your Focus with One Image

Here's how you can use **The One Image Method** to shift from problems to solutions:

1. Find Your Image:

2. Choose a picture that represents your ultimate goal or dream. It should excite and inspire you, whether it's a photo of a place, a symbol of success, or a vision of the life you want.

3. Keep It Visible:

4. Place your Image where you'll see it every day. Make it your phone background, put it on your desk, or tape it to your mirror.

5. Use It as a Filter:

6. Whenever you face a challenge or decision, ask yourself: *Does this move me closer to my Vision?*

7. Refocus Daily:

8. Please spend a few moments each morning looking at your Image and imagining the life it represents. Let it anchor your thoughts and guide your actions.

## From Stuck to Solutions

Focusing on problems keeps you stuck, but focusing on solutions sets you free.

Your problems don't define you. They're just obstacles on the path to your Vision. And with **The One Image Method**, you have the clarity and tools to move past them.

So, take a moment to find your Image. Let it be a reminder of what's possible. And the next time you feel stuck, remember this story—and know that your breakthrough might be just one solution away.

# CHAPTER 4:
# Building Dreams with Focus – The Vision That Started It All

*"Clarity is freedom. Knowing what is important to you will grant you the freedom to ignore everything else."*

— James Clear

*"We have all been taught to think outside the box... but there is no box."*

— Eric Hawkins

## The Tipping Point: When Life Demands More Clarity

You're sitting at the end of a long day, scrolling through your phone, looking at other people's perfectly curated lives. You're not inspired—just exhausted. In your mind, a quiet voice whispers, *When is it my turn?*

You've worked hard your whole life. You've sacrificed, pushed forward, and done everything you were supposed to do. But despite all that effort, something feels off.

It's like running on a treadmill—pouring your energy into moving forward—but you're still in the same place at the end of the day.

The dreams you once held so tightly seem farther away now than ever. You tell yourself, One day, I'll figure it out. One day, I'll have the time and energy to create the life I've always wanted.

But here's the truth: One day doesn't come unless you make it come.

This chapter isn't about chasing your dreams. It's about creating focus, finding clarity, and anchoring your dreams in something so powerful that it pulls you forward—even when everything else is holding you back.

It's about The One Image Method.

## Why the Old Ways Don't Work

When I was stuck, I tried everything they told me— goal-setting exercises, productivity hacks, and even traditional vision boards. None of it worked.

Sylvia and I had big dreams. We wanted to build a tiny house village, live with freedom and purpose, and create a legacy for our family. But every day felt like a whirlwind of responsibilities: raising kids, managing businesses, and trying to stay afloat financially.

We thought we'd get there if we worked harder. But no matter how hard we pushed, the life we wanted always felt out of reach.

We sat down to create a vision board one night, desperate for control. We grabbed scissors, glue, and a stack of magazines, cutting out pictures of everything we thought we wanted:

1. The perfect house.

2. A new car.

3. Dream vacations.

4. Smiling families.

At first, it felt exciting. Seeing all those images together gave us a sense of possibility. But the more we looked at it, the more overwhelming it felt.

Here's the problem with traditional vision boards: **they're cluttered.** They don't reflect the life you truly want—they reflect a collage of disconnected desires that may not even align with your values.

We realized our vision board wasn't helping us focus— it was making us feel scattered. That night, we tore it down and started over.

## The Birth of the One-Image Method

Instead of filling a board with dozens of pictures, we chose just one.

We found an image of a tiny house village surrounded by trees, walkways, and a fire pit. It wasn't just a picture of houses—it symbolized everything we wanted: simplicity, freedom, connection, and purpose.

Every time we looked at it, we saw more than the village. We saw couples on porches, mornings filled with quiet peace, and evenings gathered around the fire pit. We saw the life we wanted to create, and for the first time, it felt real.

This was the beginning of the **One Image Method.**

Unlike traditional vision boards, this wasn't just something we hung on a wall and forgot about. We carried this Image with us everywhere—on our phones, tucked under the visor of our car, in the RV. Every time we saw it, it reminded us of what we were working toward. It wasn't just a picture; it was a promise.

*Want to see our One-Image we carried with us?*

## The Breakthrough You've Been Waiting For

Let's get real for a moment. You've been stuck, and you know it. Maybe you've told yourself it's because life is too hectic, you don't have enough time, or you'll "get to it later."

But deep down, there's a truth you haven't faced yet.

It's not the distractions, the time, or the obstacles keeping you stuck. Somewhere along the way, you stopped believing your dream was possible.

You let fear, doubt, and disappointment settle in like uninvited guests.

But I'm here to tell you—you can't afford to stay here any longer.

The life you want will not wait. It won't magically appear one day when everything lines up perfectly. Starting today, it's up to you to reach out and take control of your Vision.

You've got dreams that have been tugging at you for years. That dream career. That life of peace and freedom. That version of yourself who shows up every day with purpose and confidence. It's all still waiting for you.

And it starts with **one moment of clarity**. One Image that defines everything you're working toward.

## Your One Image Is More Than a Picture

It reminds us that we can bridge that gap no matter how far we feel from our dreams. It's a beacon of hope that cuts through the noise of everyday life.

When you're faced with exhaustion and doubt—when life throws yet another curveball—your One Image is there to ground you. It whispers:

You're stronger than this moment.

You're capable of more than you think.

Keep going.

Because the truth is, you don't need perfect conditions to start. You don't need to have all the answers or even believe 100% in yourself right now. All you need is a vivid vision that refuses to let you quit.

## It's Time to Take Action

So, here's my challenge to you: Stop waiting. Stop thinking. **Start seeing.**

Close your eyes right now. Picture the life you want as if you're already living it. See the people around you, hear the sounds, feel the joy and peace in your heart.

What does that life look like?

Now, open your eyes and capture that Vision. Find a single image that embodies it—an image that will anchor you in your pursuit of that dream. Save it on your phone, print it, and carry it everywhere.

From this moment forward, let it guide you. Let it shape your choices, your energy, and your actions.

Every time fear creeps in, every time the voice of doubt tells you to quit, return to that Image.

*Does this move me closer to my Vision?* If the answer is yes, take the step. If the answer is no, let it go.

You're not stuck anymore. You're on a path. And with this Vision in hand, you're already transforming your life—one powerful choice at a time.

## Hope Meets Action

You don't need permission to chase your dreams. You don't need someone to tell you it's your turn.

This is your moment. Right here. Right now.

The life you've dreamed of is waiting for you to claim it. Don't let another day pass without moving closer to it.

You have everything you need. All left is for you to believe in and act on it.

# CHAPTER 5:
# The Power of One Image –
# Our Tiny House Village

*"Clarity is freedom. Know what is important to you, and it will grant you the freedom to ignore everything else."*

*— James Clear*

*"You can't live the life you've imagined without letting go of the life you're stuck in."*

*— Eric Hawkins*

## The Ache of Unlived Dreams

Have you ever looked around and thought, *Is this it?* Maybe you've worked hard and built a life that looks successful on the outside—house, career, family—but deep down, something feels off. You wake up feeling like you missed the path meant for you.

That sense of discontent had a name for Sylvia and me: Cape Charles, Virginia. We stumbled upon the town in 1997 during one of those meandering drives to escape the pressures of everyday life.

Cape Charles was unlike anywhere else. It was quiet and serene, with shallow, peaceful beaches perfect for our kids and sunsets that stretched across the horizon like a living masterpiece.

Sylvia, and the kids fell in love with the town instantly. Whenever we visited, she'd say, *"We should buy a house here. This is the life we've been searching for."* I saw it, too. I imagined us raising our family in the stillness of small-town living, leaving behind the chaos and grind we had grown used to.

But fear held me back. I masked it as practicality. The houses were in rough shape, and the investment was risky. *What if we stretched ourselves too thin? What if it didn't work?* Every logical excuse was rooted in one truth: I was afraid to leap.

So, we stayed stuck. We watched opportunity after opportunity slip away. Homes that could have been ours were sold and restored by others. Each missed chance became a painful reminder of how fear had stolen from us.

Years passed, and we carried that ache in our hearts. But by 2021, something inside us shifted. We had faced enough setbacks to understand that fear would never leave—it would always show up when dreams were on the line.

This time, we chose to move forward anyway, with faith as our guide.

## Why We Went Tiny

Our life wasn't working. We had a large house and all the responsibilities that came with it. We loved our home, but we were not enjoying it. We were working so hard running our business that we were like two ships passing in the night. It looked like we had it all together from the outside, but inside, we were drowning. The house wasn't a home anymore. It was a place to lay our heads to get ready for the next day.

Sylvia and I had become partners in survival mode, stuck in a cycle of daily obligations. Our dreams had faded into the background.

I hadn't enjoyed my back yard in years. In one of my failed attempts to some sort of normal life about 5 years earlier, I had bought a gas grill, a nice one too. I had this belief that I was going to force myself to take time off to really enjoy my backyard and relax. I said it was a failed attempt because it's all covered up and ready to go in the backyard. So I decided I am going to use my grill today, hell or high water, today is the day. When I took the cover off, I was surprised to see the stainless steel still looked good, so I had high hopes, until I opened the top. That's when I saw that the ants had created a whole city in there. They had taken over the whole inside of the grill. Cmon man, really? My son wanted to clean them out as he was ready for some burgers. On the other hand, I was mesmerized by how these little ants were using something I was underutilizing.

I stood there, staring at the grill, at the tiny city the ants had built in a place I had neglected. They had found purpose in something I had let sit idle for years. The irony wasn't lost on me. Here I was, the one who had bought the grill with good intentions, yet these ants had used it better than I ever did.

As I brushed them away, I felt something deeper stirring. This wasn't just about the grill—it was about my life. I had built something impressive on the outside, yet inside, I had let it sit, unused, stagnant. Just like the grill, just like my backyard, just like my dreams.

That realization followed me inside, lingering in my chest as I sat down at the kitchen table with Sylvia. The weight of it all, the house, the business, the constant grind—it was suffocating. I looked at her, and I knew she felt it too.

I broke the silence. "We can't keep living like this," I said quietly.

We couldn't.

I broke the silence one night as we sat at the kitchen table. "We can't keep living like this," I said quietly.

We couldn't. The weight of it all—the house, the business, the routine that no longer served us— pressed down on us from every angle. Something had to give.

I exhaled, gripping the edge of the table. *OK,* I told myself. *I would downsize my company.* That part made sense— I was carrying too much, and it was time to let some of it go. But the house?

That was different. Selling it outright felt too final, too permanent. What if this was just a phase? What if we regretted it?

Instead, we took a step that felt bold but safer. We rented the house to long-term tenants, holding onto it just in case. Then, we packed what little we could fit into our travel trailer, stripping life down to the essentials. This wasn't just downsizing—it was redefining. This was our version of living tiny.

It was a bold move, and it terrified us. We were letting go of the material markers of success that we thought defined us.

But in that space of letting go, something unexpected happened. Tiny living stripped away the distractions that had consumed our lives. Without a big house to maintain and clutter to manage, we found clarity—about who we were, what we wanted, and what mattered.

Our marriage began to heal in ways we didn't know it needed. We started dreaming together again. We talked about what we wanted the next chapter of our lives to look like—not just for us but for the people we wanted to serve. We began our long walks that eventually turned into hiking; I reconnected with my wife doing this. There is something about being outside in nature, walking and talking even in our silent moments while walking; we were reconnecting and healing. We even began to travel more.

Tiny living allowed us to envision something bigger: a tiny house village where others could experience the same peace and simplicity that had transformed us.

## Preparation Through the Struggles

Remember that your struggles today will shape you for something far greater than you can see.

While living our version of living tiny, we got into Airbnb as a short-term rental host. We started and managed 19 short-term rental listings. The challenges were endless—broken appliances, double bookings, late-night guest calls. At the time, it felt like we were constantly putting out fires. But in hindsight, those struggles were preparing us. They taught us resilience, problemsolving, and how to create experiences that people value.

We wouldn't have been ready for what came next without those lessons.

## The Moment Everything Changed

It was a simple drive across the Chesapeake Bay Bridge Tunnel—something we often did to clear our minds. The expanse of the ocean on either side always had a calming effect, reminding us of how vast and full of possibilities the world is.

Usually, we turned left toward the familiar streets of Cape Charles. But that day, something nudged us to turn right. We didn't have a destination; we just wanted to explore.

As we drove, Sylvia suddenly shouted, *"Stop the car!"*

I hit the brakes, startled. To the left of us, hidden behind a wall of overgrown trees, was an abandoned and forgotten property. Ten crumbling structures stood in the shadows, barely visible under neglect. The roofs were caving in, windows shattered, vines choking the walls. It was a scene straight out of a horror movie.

My first instinct was to drive away. This place was a disaster. *Too much work, too much risk.*

But Sylvia saw something else entirely. She reached into the car's visor and pulled out the One Image we had carried since our tiny living journey began. It was a picture of a thriving tiny house village surrounded by trees and warmth.

*"This is it,"* she whispered, her voice filled with certainty. *"This is the dream."*

*This is how we found them*

At that moment, the ruins before me transformed. Through the lens of our Vision, I saw what Sylvia saw—a foundation waiting to be restored. Families gathered around fire pits, couples reconnecting on porches, a village where life slowed down to what truly mattered.

Without that Vision, we would have driven past it like everyone else. But with it, we knew this was where we were meant to build.

## Bringing the Vision to Life

Transforming that property was one of the hardest things we'd ever done. The physical labor, the financial strain, the endless setbacks—they pushed us to the brink.

There were nights when I lay awake, consumed by doubt. *What if this doesn't work? What if we fail?*

But I looked at our One Image every time those thoughts crept in. It reminded me why we started. It anchored us in the dream we had carried for so long.

Slowly, the pieces came together. The land was cleared, the structures repaired, and **Cape Charles Tiny Livin'** began to take shape.

What once felt impossible became a place of transformation—not just for us, but for everyone who visits.

## The Power of One Vision

Let me talk to you—not just the version of you working hard to keep life running but the part of you that still dreams.

I know what it's like to feel like life is slipping away while caught in an endless cycle of responsibility. You've put your dreams on the shelf because everything else—the bills, the obligations, the expectations—feels more urgent.

But deep down, that ache you feel isn't going away. It's the part of you that knows you were made for more. It's your soul saying, *Wake up. Please don't give up on me.*

This is where *One Vision* becomes your lifeline.

## Your Vision is Calling

The distractions, doubts, and setbacks will always be there. But so will your dream. It's time to listen to that inner voice telling you that there's still time to build the life you've imagined.

So, find your One Image and let it guide you through every challenge, just as it guided us.

Because your story is still being written—and the next chapter is yours to create.

# CHAPTER 6:

# The PATH Framework – Turning Vision Into Action

*"Do not wait for the perfect moment. Take the moment and make it perfect."*

— *Sarah Ban Breathnach*

*"A clear vision is your compass, but even the clearest compass needs a map to guide you through the journey."*

— *Eric Hawkins*

## From Vision to Action

Your One Image is your anchor. It represents everything you want—your dreams, your aspirations, the life you know you're meant to live. But a vision won't manifest itself, no matter how clear or inspiring.

Here's the truth: having a vision without a plan is like trying to build a house without blueprints. You might gather the materials, but you'll only have a pile of dreams without structure.

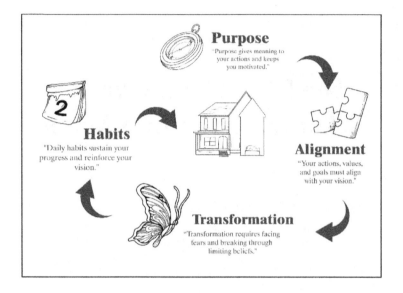

That's why the PATH Framework exists—to take your One Image from inspiration to action, from an idea to a reality you can live with daily.

## Why Do So Many Dreams Fade?

How many times have you set a goal only to abandon it a few weeks later? How often do you feel inspired, only to lose steam when life gets in the way?

It's not because you lack drive or capability. The problem is that most people rely on motivation alone, which is fleeting.

What you need isn't just excitement; it's a system.

The **PATH Framework** provides that system. It's a step-by-step guide to transforming your One Image into a tangible, unstoppable force.

## The Four Pillars of the PATH Framework

The PATH Framework stands on four interconnected pillars:

1. **P**urpose – The emotional heartbeat of your journey.

2. **A**lignment – The synchronization of your life with your Vision.

3. **T**ransformation – The inner growth required to achieve your dreams.

4. **H**abits – The small, consistent actions that sustain success.

Your One Image is at the center of it all. Each pillar builds on its clarity and focus, ensuring your efforts aren't scattered but deliberate and meaningful.

# Pillar 1: Purpose – The Emotional Heartbeat

The purpose is the foundation of everything. It's your "why"—the driving force that keeps you going when the road gets hard.

## Your One Image as Your Purpose Anchor

Think of your **One Image** as the emotional heart of your purpose. You're reminded of what truly matters every time you look at it. It's not just a picture—it's the story of your future, captured in a single moment.

## The Science of Purpose

When you connect your goals to a meaningful purpose, your brain releases **dopamine**—the neurotransmitter responsible for motivation and pleasure. This creates a positive feedback loop: the more you focus on your purpose, the more motivated you feel to take action.

This isn't just theory—it's how your brain is wired. Purpose turns effort into joy and obstacles into challenges you're ready to overcome.

## Reflection Exercise: Finding Your Why

Take 10 minutes to answer the following questions:

1. What does my **One Image** represent, and why does it matter to you?

2. How will achieving this Vision improve my life and the lives of those I care about?

3. What do I want my life to reflect five years from now?

Write your answers down and revisit them daily. Pair them with your **One Image** to create a powerful emotional anchor.

# Pillar 2: Alignment – Syncing Your Life with Your Vision

There comes a moment when you realize that your path doesn't match the life you imagined. It's subtle at first—you feel drained by tasks that don't matter. You wonder why, despite your hard work, fulfillment remains out of reach.

Alignment isn't about doing more—it's about doing the *right* things. It's about matching your daily choices to the Vision in your heart.

### Signs You're Out of Alignment

Ask yourself these questions:

1. Are you waking up each day with a clear sense of where you're going, or are you caught in the storm of "busy"?

2. Is your calendar filled with activities that align with your dreams, or are you living by someone else's expectations?

3. Do your surroundings inspire you to take action on your Vision, or do they add to your stress?

## Creating Alignment

Imagine walking down a winding road, but someone pulls you in a different direction every few steps. One person says, *"Come this way—this is where success is!"* Another whispers, *"You should focus on this instead!"*

Soon, you're wandering in circles, exhausted but no closer to your destination.

Alignment frees you from that chaos. It's about focusing on *your* path and tuning out the noise that doesn't serve you.

## Practical Steps to Create Alignment

1. Audit Your Time

1. Look at your daily schedule. Are your actions supporting your **One Image**, or are they distractions disguised as productivity?

2. What can you eliminate to make room for what truly matters?

2. Evaluate Your Environment

1. Declutter your physical and mental space. Add elements that inspire you— pictures, affirmations, or symbols that reflect your Vision.

3. Examine Your Relationships

1. Are the people around you supporting or draining you?

2. Seek those who inspire and uplift you. Let go of relationships that pull you away from your purpose.

4. Set a Daily Intention

1. Start each morning by revisiting your **One Image**. Ask yourself: What is one thing I can do today that moves me closer to this Vision?

2. Small, consistent actions will create unstoppable momentum.

## Pillar 3: Transformation – Becoming the Person Who Achieves the Vision

Here's a truth that's hard to face: the person you are today isn't the person who will achieve your Vision. Transformation isn't optional—it's necessary.

### Facing Your Inner Roadblocks

Transformation begins with identifying the fears and limiting beliefs that are holding you back:

1. I'm not good enough.

2. I don't have what it takes.

3. What if I fail?

These thoughts aren't just obstacles—they're growth opportunities. When confronting them, you're rewiring your brain, shifting from fear to possibility.

### Practical Transformation Exercise

1. Write down one fear or limiting belief you have.

2. Challenge it by writing a counter-belief that reflects possibility.

3. 3 . Example: Replace "I'm not good enough" with "I am capable of learning and growing."

4. Take one small action that aligns with your new belief.

## Pillar 4: Habits – The Foundation of Sustainable Success

Habits turn short-term effort into long-term success. They're the foundation that keeps your Vision alive every day.

### The Science of Habits

Habits work because they automate success. By creating consistent routines, you free up mental energy for bigger decisions.

Psychologists describe habits as loops consisting of:

1. **Cue:** A trigger that initiates the habit.

2. **Routine:** The action itself.

3. **Reward:** The positive reinforcement that sustains the habit.

### Building Habits That Stick

1. **Start Small** – Choose one habit that aligns with your **One Image**.

2. **Be Consistent** – Repeat it daily until it becomes automatic.

3. **Celebrate Wins** – Acknowledge even the slightest progress.

## The PATH Framework in Action

The **PATH Framework** isn't just a guide—it's a transformation. When you pair it with your **One Image**, you create a system that keeps you moving forward, no matter what life throws your way.

1. **Purpose** keeps you motivated.

2. **Alignment** keeps you focused.

3. **Transformation** helps you grow.

4. **Habits** sustain your success.

# Your Next Step

Look at your **One Image**. Let it remind you of what's possible. Then, take one small step today to align your life with your Vision.

The journey isn't always easy, but with the **PATH Framework,** you have everything you need to make your Vision unstoppable.

Turn the page. Let's build the future you deserve.

# CHAPTER 7:

# Breaking Through the Resistance – Overcoming Objections to Transformation

*"Most of us have two lives: the life we live and the unlived life within us. Between the two stands Resistance."*

— *Steven Pressfield*

*"Resistance isn't a wall—it's a test to see if you'll fight for the life you deserve."*

— *Eric Hawkins*

## The Whisper of Doubt

It starts quietly. That voice in your head says, "This won't work for me. It's too simple. It's too unrealistic. I've tried and failed before."

You're not alone in feeling this way. Doubt is a natural reaction when stepping into something new that challenges the familiar patterns you've clung to. It's easier to stick with what you know —even if it's not working—than to embrace the vulnerability of change.

But here's the truth: Resistance isn't your enemy. It's the last barrier standing between you and the life you want. Let's break it down, objection by objection, and reveal how the One Image Method and PATH Framework can help you push through.

## Objection 1: "This is just wishful thinking."

You're skeptical, and that's fair. The world is full of promises that sound too good to be true— quick fixes that leave you more stuck than before.

But this isn't about luck or hoping for the best. It's about **clarity, focus, and deliberate action**.

## The Science Behind the One-Image Method

Your brain is designed to prioritize what you tell it is essential. This is where the **Reticular Activating System (RAS)**comes in—a bundle of neurons in your brainstem that filters information based on your focus.

When you create **One Image**, you're programming your brain to notice opportunities, ideas, and connections that align with your Vision. It's like buying a red car and suddenly seeing red cars everywhere—they were always there, but now your brain knows to pay attention.

### Your Action Step

1. Find your **One Image** and make it visible.

2. Pair it with this question: What's one small step I can take today to move closer to this Vision?

## Objection 2: "I don't have time."

Life is busy—there's no denying that. Between work, family, and endless to-do lists, carving out time for anything new feels impossible.

But here's the thing: The One Image Method doesn't require more time—it helps you make the most of your time.

### The Time Reality Check

The average person spends over three hours a day on their phone. Imagine if even a fraction of that time was spent focusing on your Vision.

You don't need hours of free time with the One Image Method. You need **a few intentional moments each day** to reconnect with your purpose.

**Your Action Step**

1. Save your **One Image** as your phone or desktop background.

2. Every time you see it, ask yourself: Am I spending my time in a way that aligns with this Vision?

# Objection 3: "I've tried things like this before, and they didn't work."

It's frustrating. You've set goals, made plans, and given your best effort, only to return to where you started.

But here's the difference: The One Image Method isn't just about setting goals—it's about anchoring your focus and aligning your actions daily.

## The Story Reframed: What If I Didn't Have My One Vision?

What if I didn't have that One Vision with me the day we stumbled upon those broken-down homes hidden behind trees?

What if I'd been like all the others—those countless people who drove past it every day without a second glance, seeing nothing but ruin and neglect?

I can tell you precisely what would have happened. I would've kept driving. I would've looked at that property, with its shattered windows and caved-in roofs, and thought, This is a nightmare: too much work, money, and risk. I would've let fear, disguised as logic, talk me out of it just like I had so many times before.

Without my One Vision, I never would have seen the potential buried beneath the overgrowth. I never would've seen the dream hiding in plain sight—the dream of a place that could become a sanctuary for others seeking peace and transformation.

But that day, I did have my One Vision. Sylvia pulled it out right there in the car. And in that moment, it was like a switch flipped. The wreckage didn't scare me anymore. I didn't see decay; I saw possibility. That Image reminded me of everything I had been working toward—the life we had dreamed of, the clarity that tiny living had given us.

But here's the thing. It wasn't just the One Vision that prepared me to see it.

What if I hadn't spent years building those 19 Airbnb listings? What if I hadn't struggled through late-night calls from guests, broken appliances, and the chaos of running multiple properties? I wouldn't have known how to handle the challenges that lay ahead.

What if we hadn't built my wife's salon, turning her Vision into a thriving business? I wouldn't have known how to make our dream a reality.

What if we hadn't decided to live tiny—leaving behind everything we thought defined as success, only to discover how much clarity and peace come from letting go? I wouldn't have been open to something this unconventional, this crazy.

Every experience that stretched and tested me prepared me for that moment. You see, sometimes, when life feels like it's falling apart, it's falling into place. What feels like failure, rejection, or frustration is often life—or God—working on you, not against you. I didn't realize it then, but all the obstacles and doubts shaped me into someone who could build something greater than I had ever imagined.

Now, let's talk about you for a second.

What if the reason you feel stuck isn't because you're failing but because you're being shaped? What if the struggles you're facing prepare you for a moment you can't see yet—a moment where everything suddenly makes sense?

Without that Vision, you might miss it. You might keep driving past your dream without realizing it's there, waiting for you to claim it. Don't let that happen.

Hold your Vision close. Let it guide you through the storms of doubt and fear. It reminds you daily that what you're building is worth the struggle.

Because one day, you'll look back and realize it was never just about the dream. It was about becoming the person who could bring it to life.

## Your Action Step

1.  Ask yourself: What can I do differently this time?

2.  Simplify your approach and focus on what truly matters.

# Objection 4: "What if I fail?"

This might be the most strenuous objection because it's rooted in fear of failing, wasting time, and proving the doubters wrong.

But here's the truth: **Failure isn't the end—it's feedback.** Every step, even the ones that don't go as planned, teaches you something valuable.

## Reframing Failure

Think of failure as a staircase. Each step brings you closer to your goal, no matter how small. Even if you stumble, you're still moving upward.

Fear of failure only has power if you let it stop you. But when you reframe failure as growth, you realize that **every effort moves you forward.**

## Your Action Step

1. Reframe your fear by asking yourself: What's scarier—failing or staying exactly where I am for the next five years?

2. Write down one small action you can take today, even if it feels imperfect.

## You Are Stronger Than Resistance

Resistance is a test—it challenges you to prove how much your dreams matter to you. It will show up every time you push for something greater. But with the **One Image Method** and the **PATH Framework**, you have the tools to fight back.

Every time you feel doubt creeping in, return to your **One Image**. Let it remind you why you started this journey and that you can break through.

## Your Next Move

Resistance is not here to defeat you. It's here to see how committed you are to your Vision.

Take a deep breath. Look at your **One Image**.

Decide today that no obstacle, no fear, and no excuse will stand in your way.

You've come too far to stop now.

Turn the page. Let's move forward with unstoppable momentum.

*With God's hand, hard work, and an unwavering vision, we turned dreams into reality—one tiny house at a time. What once was overlooked is now a vibrant sanctuary of possibility. Cape Charles Tiny Livin' isn't just a place; it's proof that faith, grit, and a clear vision can create something extraordinary.*

# CHAPTER 8:

# Discovery Beyond Feeling Stuck

*"In the middle of every difficulty lies opportunity."*
— *Albert Einstein*

*"Feeling stuck isn't a failure. It's your roots growing deeper, preparing you for your next breakthrough."*
— *Eric Hawkins*

## A Journey of Discovery

Close your eyes for a moment. Take a deep breath and let the tension in your shoulders release. Picture yourself standing at the edge of a dense forest. You can't see the other side, but you know that the life you've been dreaming of is beyond those trees—a life of clarity, purpose, and freedom.

The forest feels intimidating, doesn't it? The unknown always does. But here's what I want you to know: **the path through that forest exists**. And you've already taken the first steps.

## The Weight of Feeling Stuck

If you've ever felt stuck, you know how heavy it can be. Like quicksand, it pulls you deeper the more you struggle. The weight of doubt, frustration, and fear presses on you, whispering, *"This isn't working." It may be time to give up.*

But here's the truth: feeling stuck doesn't mean you're failing. It means you're growing.

## The Misunderstood Work of Growth

People feel stuck because they try something long enough to say it doesn't work. They dip their toes into a new routine, mindset, or dream, hoping for instant transformation. When it doesn't come fast enough, they retreat, telling themselves, *"See? I knew it wasn't going to work."*

But growth doesn't announce itself with fireworks. It doesn't shout, "Look! You're changing!" Growth is often quiet, hidden beneath the surface. Like a seed planted in the soil, transformation begins out of sight.

## The Seed Analogy

When you plant a seed in the ground, you water it, give it sunlight, and wait. But for weeks, maybe months, nothing seems to happen. The soil looks the same, and the ground is unbroken, so it's easy to believe nothing is happening.

But underground, that seed is transforming. Its roots are growing deeper, spreading wider, anchoring it firmly into the earth. Only when those roots are strong do they sprout breakthroughs, reaching for the light.

Your life works the same way. The times when you feel stuck are the times when **your roots are growing**. The lessons you're learning, the resilience you're building, and the clarity you're gaining are all happening beneath the surface.

"I know what it feels like to wake up every day and wonder if things will ever improve. Maybe you've built a life that looks good on paper—a steady job, responsibilities, perhaps even a beautiful home—but inside, you feel empty. You feel trapped by your obligations, weighed down by fear, and disconnected from the person you once dreamed of becoming.

I want you to know something that took me years to understand: You're not broken. You're not failing. Feeling stuck doesn't mean you've reached a dead end. It's a signal—an opportunity to listen to your heart and make a shift. I know this because I've lived it. Fear paralyzed me, telling myself stories about why I couldn't take the next step. I told myself I lacked time, money, or courage. I know the pain of pushing forward only to feel like you're running in place.

But I also know the power of having a vision—that moment when everything changes—not because life suddenly becomes easy but because you finally see that you deserve more. And the truth is, you do. You deserve joy, fulfillment, and the life you've dreamed about in secret.

I won't tell you this is easy—transformation never is— but I can tell you that every single step forward is worth it. You don't have to figure it all out today. Start with one thing. Start by believing that this isn't the end for you—it's the beginning of something greater."

# The Discovery in "Stuck" Moments

Think back to a time in your life when you overcame something hard, maybe a breakup, a financial struggle, or a career challenge. At the time, it felt impossible. But looking back, you can see how that experience shaped you. It made you stronger, wiser, and more capable.

That's the beauty of stuck moments: they're not the end but the beginning of discovery.

### **Breaking Through Analysis Paralysis**

I remember sitting at my desk, staring at the financials of the business I had built with my own hands. I should have felt proud. This company had been my everything—my security, my identity, and proof that I could succeed. But instead of pride, I felt suffocated. I was trapped in a life I no longer recognized as my own.

The company was thriving, but I wasn't. Each day felt like a slow erosion of my dreams. The work that once gave me purpose now drained every joy I had left. Yet, the idea of letting go terrified me. I kept thinking: *What if I'm wrong? What if I'm throwing everything away?*

I became stuck in a loop of analysis paralysis. Every decision felt like a potential disaster. I couldn't sleep. I couldn't focus. I was paralyzed by the fear of making the wrong choice.

You know that feeling, don't you? When your life is filled with responsibilities, deadlines, and obligations—so much that you can't even remember what it feels like to dream anymore. When the fear of failing or wasting time is louder than the voice urging you to move forward.

I didn't know it then, but I was at a crossroads between who I was and who I was meant to be. #### **The Turning Point**

It all changed the day I turned to my One Image. I had carried that Image with me since my tiny living journey began. It represented freedom, clarity, and the life I knew I was destined for. I looked at that picture—looked at it— and something inside me cracked open.

I saw it clearly now—my HVAC company was no longer the path to my destination. It had carried me this far, served its purpose, and provided for my family. But holding onto it out of fear wouldn't bring me any closer to the life I truly wanted. It was time to let go.

The weight of that truth settled in, and my chest tightened. Tears welled in my eyes—not just for the business, but for the version of myself that had built it, depended on it, and found identity in it. I wasn't just selling a company; I was releasing a part of me that had clung to security, mistaking it for freedom.

But in that moment, I understood something profound—staying stuck was scarier than moving forward.

So I made the call. I sold the company. And while it wasn't easy, it helped that I was handing it to someone I trusted with my life. That made the goodbye just a little easier.

And let me tell you, it wasn't instant relief. There were moments of doubt, nights when fear tried to creep back in. But every time it did, I returned to my One Image. I reminded myself that I was building something greater.

What happened next still amazes me. The clarity that had eluded me for years suddenly became my reality. New opportunities—ones I hadn't dared to imagine—began to unfold. I wasn't trapped anymore. I was free.

What About You?

I want you to pause for a moment. What's the thing you're clinging to out of fear? Is it a job, a relationship, or a comfort zone that no longer serves you?

You already know what it is. You feel it deep in your gut every time you wake up, dreading the day ahead. Every time you tell yourself, *I can't do this forever.*

Here's the truth: Staying stuck won't protect you. It won't keep you safe. It will only rob you of the life you were meant to live.

But you don't have to stay stuck. You can choose a different path. I know it's scary. I see the doubt feels like a heavy weight on your chest. But the One Image Method isn't just some motivational gimmick. It's your lifeline.

When you carry your One Image, you have a vision that will guide you through the fear. It will remind you why you're doing this and show you that your breakthrough is waiting on the other side of your fear.

The Life You Want Is Within Reach

I can't promise that the journey will be easy. You will face setbacks, challenges, and moments of deep uncertainty. But I can promise this: Every step you take in alignment with your Vision will bring you closer to the life you deserve.

You have a choice right now. You can stay where you are, trapped by fear and indecision. Or you can take that first small step toward freedom, purpose, and joy.

Look at your One Image. Let it speak to you. Let it remind you that you were made for more. This is your moment to break through the resistance and create a life you'll be proud of.

You don't have to wait anymore. The life you've dreamed of is waiting for you. It's time to claim it.

## Reframing "Stuck" as Growth

Feeling stuck isn't a failure. It's preparation. It's the roots growing beneath the soil. It's the seed transforming into something ready to bloom.

What might be working on me right now?

You may learn patience while waiting for a dream to unfold, build strength as you navigate a tough season, or gain clarity about what you truly want.

Whatever it is, trust that it's happening for a reason.

## Visualizing the Breakthrough

Let's do an exercise together. Close your eyes and picture the life you want—not the vague idea of success, but the specific details: the house, the relationships, the career, the joy. Picture your **One Image**—that singular representation of everything you're working toward. See it in vivid detail, like you're already living it.

Now imagine the path that brought you there—the small steps you took, the moments when you wanted to give up but didn't, and the overwhelming challenges that made you stronger. See yourself standing in that life, looking back at the journey that got you there. Feel the pride, the gratitude, the fulfillment.

That's what's waiting for you. And every step you take brings you closer, no matter how small.

## The Discovery of Your Purpose

I wrote this book because I know what it feels like to be stuck. Do you want more but do not know how to get it? Have you tried and failed and wondered if it's even worth it?

But I also know what's on the other side of that feeling. I've seen it in my own life and the lives of so many others. The transformation, the freedom, the joy—it's all real. And it's all possible for you.

Your **One Image** is more than a picture. It's a promise to yourself. A reminder of what you're capable of and what you deserve.

When you feel stuck, look at that Image and remember why you started. Let it pull you forward, step by step until you're living the life you've always dreamed of.

## Action Steps for Discovery

To close this chapter, here are three simple steps to turn your discovery into action:

**1.** Embrace the Process

Recognize that growth takes time. When you feel stuck, remind yourself that **your roots are growing**, preparing you for the breakthrough.

**2.** Reconnect with Your One Image

Keep it visible and present in your daily life. Let it be the anchor that keeps you focused and motivated.

**3.** Take One Small Step Today

Progress doesn't have to be significant. It just has to be consistent. What's one thing you can do right now to move closer to your Vision?

## Your Journey Ahead

The journey from stuck to unstoppable isn't always easy, but it's always worth it. Every moment of frustration, obstacle, and doubt is part of the process. They shape you into the person who can achieve your dreams.

So when you feel stuck, remember this: It's not working against you. It's working on you.

Trust the process, keep moving forward, and know that the life you've been dreaming of is closer than you think.

Let's Take the Next Step Together.

# CONCLUSION:
# You Are Unstoppable

*"The future depends on what you do today."*
— *Mahatma Gandhi*

*"You don't need permission to chase your dreams. Your Vision is your birthright. Claim it."*
— *Eric Hawkins*

## You Made It Here for a Reason

By now, you've traveled through this book with an open heart and a desire for change. You've faced your doubts, questioned your limits, and opened yourself to the possibility of something greater.

Let me say this clearly: **the fact that you're here, reading these words, means you're already unstoppable.** You've taken the most crucial step—

acknowledging that you want more and believing it's possible.

## The Journey So Far

Think about where you were when you started this journey. Maybe you felt stuck, spinning your wheels, unsure how to move forward. Life may have felt like a constant loop of busyness without progress.

Now, you're armed with clarity. You've discovered your **One Image**, the singular, powerful representation of the life you want to live. You've explored the **PATH Framework**, a proven system that transforms dreams into actionable steps. And you've learned how to overcome resistance, silence self-doubt, and stay focused despite distractions.

## Your Future Is Calling

Here's what I know to be true: transformation is a choice. And by reading this book, you've already made that choice.

But this is just the beginning. Real change happens when you take what you've learned here and put it into action—when you allow your **One Image** to guide every decision, every step, every day.

So, I want to ask you a question:

What will you do today to honor your Vision?

1. Will you create a morning routine that brings your One Image to life?

2. Will you take one bold step toward your purpose?

3. Will you release the distractions that no longer serve you?

The life you want isn't waiting for someone else to live it. **It's waiting for you.**

## An Invitation to Build Together

I didn't write this book to share my story—I wrote it because I believe in yours.

Your journey and vision matter and your success will inspire others to take their first steps.

Here's how we can continue this journey together:

1. Stay Connected: Follow me on Instagram @mrerichawkins for ongoing inspiration and

resources. Or to see what we are doing now @capecharles_tinylivin

2.  Reach Out: Message me directly—I'd love to hear how the One Image Method is helping you create your unstoppable future.

3.  Stay Connected: Follow us on Instagram to see what we are doing now @capecharles_tinylivin.

4.  Want to come visit us? www.capecharlestinylivin.com. Enter Coupon Code "One Image" for a discount on your stay

## Your Time Is Now

Close your eyes for a moment. Picture yourself standing in the center of your **One Image**. You can feel the freedom, the confidence, and the joy of living the life you've always wanted. You can hear the laughter, feel the weight lifted, and know with absolute certainty that you're exactly where you're meant to be.

That's not just a dream. That's the life you're building— step by step, decision by decision.

The only thing left to do is act.

# Final Words

Let me leave you with this: **You're not stuck anymore.
You never were.** You were waiting for the right tools, the proper clarity, and the right moment to begin.

That moment is now.

Your future is unstoppable. Your Vision is within reach. And the best part? You have everything you need to make it real.

So, take the next step. Start today. And know that I'm here, cheering you on every step of the way.

Because you're not just a dreamer.

You're a doer.

You're unstoppable.

Thank you for taking this journey. Let's build the life you've always imagined—together.

P.S. I Thought It Was Finished... But You Need to Hear This

There's something I wish someone had told me earlier in life. It could have saved me years of frustration and fear. Maybe you need to hear it, too:

The one thing you're resisting the most—the thing that makes your chest tighten and your thoughts race—that's probably the exact thing you need to do.

I know it's terrifying. I've been there. I've stood on the edge of decisions that made me feel paralyzed by fear, of what might go wrong. But let me tell you something: **nothing will change if you circulate that fear.**

You see, fear isn't the enemy. It's a guide. It shows up to guard the thresholds of your most significant transformations. The very thing you're avoiding holds the key to breaking free of what's kept you stuck.

Whether it's walking away from a toxic job, speaking your truth, or chasing a dream you buried long ago, fear points you to where you need to grow.

The longer you run from it, the tighter its grip gets. But when you face it head-on, something shifts. You realize that fear has no power other than the power you give it.

**Do the Thing.** Whatever it is.

Make the phone call.

Say yes to the opportunity.

Take the risk.

Your mind will flood you with all the reasons it won't work, but let me tell you, the real danger isn't failure. **The real danger is waking up five years from now in the same place, wondering why you didn't try.**

I'll be honest with you: it won't always be easy. You'll face setbacks. There will be days when the Vision feels out of reach. But I promise you this—when you stop avoiding what scares you, you'll unlock a strength you didn't know you had.

## Your Next Step

Look at yourself right now and ask, What is the one thing I've been avoiding?

You already know the answer.

Here's your next step: **Take one small action toward it today.** Not tomorrow. Not next week. **Today.**

I Believe in You

You've come this far—don't stop now. Your freedom, transformation, and dreams are all waiting on the other side of that fear.

Let this be the moment you decide to stop holding yourself back.

The life you've always wanted? **It's yours to claim.**

Now go get it.

Made in the USA
Las Vegas, NV
20 March 2025

19823717R10056